REPUBLICANS

AND

DEMOCRATS

MARIEL & JONATHAN BARD

PowerKiDS
press™
New York

Published in 2020 by The Rosen Publishing Group, Inc.
29 East 21st Street, New York, NY 10010

First Edition

Editor: Jane Katirgis
Book Design: Tanya Dellaccio

Photo Credits: Cover (right), pp. 13, 15 (main) Everett Historical/Shutterstock.com; cover (left), pp. 7 (Founding Fathers), 17 (Lyndon B. Johnson) Bettmann/Getty Images; p. 5 (main) Alex Wong/Getty Images News/Getty Images; p. 5 (inset) https://upload.wikimedia.org/wikipedia/commons/6/6c/Constitution_of_the_United_States%2C_page_1.jpg; p. 7 (Alexander Hamilton) https://upload.wikimedia.org/wikipedia/commons/0/05/Alexander_Hamilton_portrait_by_John_Trumbull_1806.jpg; p. 7 (Thomas Jefferson) https://upload.wikimedia.org/wikipedia/commons/0/07/Official_Presidential_portrait_of_Thomas_Jefferson_%28by_Rembrandt_Peale%2C_1800%29.jpg; p. 9 (Democrat and Republican symbols) SFerdon/Shutterstock.com; p. 9 (Andrew Jackson) https://upload.wikimedia.org/wikipedia/commons/4/43/Andrew_jackson_head.jpg; p. 11 https://upload.wikimedia.org/wikipedia/commons/9/98/Republican_presidential_ticket_1864b.jpg; p. 15 (FDR) https://upload.wikimedia.org/wikipedia/commons/3/30/FDR_1944_Color_Portrait.tif; p. 17 (Grand Coulee Dam) Edmund Lowe Photography/Shutterstock.com; p. 19 (debate) Joseph Scherschel/The LIFE Picture Collection/Getty Images; p. 19 (family watching TV) Time Life Pictures/The LIFE Picture Collection/Getty Images; p. 21 (Supreme Court justices) Diana Walker/the LIFE Images Collection/Getty Images; p. 21 (Sandra Day O'Connor) Courtesy of the National Archives; p. 23 Dirck Halstead/The LIFE Images Collection/Getty Images; p. 25 https://upload.wikimedia.org/wikipedia/commons/9/98/Aldrin_Apollo_11_original.jpg; p. 27 Douglas Graham/CQ-Roll Call Group/Getty Images; p. 29 Hill Street Studios/Blend Images/Getty Images.

Cataloging-in-Publication Data

Names: Bard, Mariel. | Bard, Jonathan.
Title: Republicans and Democrats / Mariel and Jonathan Bard.
Description: New York : PowerKids Press, 2019. | Series: Opponents in American history | Includes glossary and index.
Identifiers: ISBN 9781538345467 (pbk.) | ISBN 9781538343708 (library bound) | ISBN 9781538345474 (6pack)
Subjects: LCSH: Republican Party (U.S. : 1854-)-Juvenile literature. | Democratic Party (U.S.)-Juvenile literature. | United States-Politics and government-20th century-Juvenile literature.
Classification: LCC JK226.B36 2019 | DDC 324.2734-dc23

Manufactured in the United States of America

CPSIA Compliance Information: Batch #CSPK19. For Further Information contact Rosen Publishing, New York, New York at 1-800-237-9932

CONTENTS

WHAT IS A POLITICAL PARTY?

Each year, Americans vote in local, state, or national elections. The candidates running for office all want to represent not only their towns or states but also the people of their community. To get enough support to win an election, a candidate often needs help from a political party, which is a group of people who share similar ideas and beliefs and who work together to gain control of government positions.

Political parties have two major goals: to promote candidates in elections and to write and support laws that support and enforce their ideas and beliefs. The more candidates a political party has in power, the easier it is to pass the laws they want. Today, the United States has two major political parties—the Republican Party and the Democratic Party.

WHAT IS A DEMOCRACY?

*Many people refer to the United States as a democracy. A democracy is a type of government in which citizens have elections to decide how they're governed. In America, we vote for public officials to represent us. These elected officials **debate** and create the laws we all live by. This form of government is also a **constitutional republic**.*

THE U.S. CONSTITUTION—RATIFIED, OR APPROVED—IN 1788, EXPLAINS HOW THE GOVERNMENT RUNS AND HOW POLITICIANS ARE ELECTED. YOU CAN SEE THE CONSTITUTION ON DISPLAY AT THE NATIONAL ARCHIVES IN WASHINGTON, D.C.

GET THE PARTIES STARTED

Long before today's Democrats and Republicans, other political parties held power in the United States. The first parties to form were the Federalists, led by Alexander Hamilton and formed in 1791, and the Democratic-Republicans, led by Thomas Jefferson and formed in 1792. (The latter was first called the Republican Party.)

The Federalists wanted a strong federal, or national, government, believing that it would be more effective for the new country. The Federalists were often supported by wealthy merchants, bankers, and other businessmen, mostly from the northern United States. The Democratic-Republicans disagreed. They wanted a small federal government that didn't interfere much with citizens' lives, and they believed each state should be in charge of its own citizens. Democratic-Republicans were supported mostly by farmers and planters.

GEORGE WASHINGTON

JEFFERSON AND HAMILTON WERE MEMBERS OF GEORGE WASHINGTON'S CABINET, PICTURED HERE.

HEAD TO HEAD

The two party leaders, Hamilton and Jefferson, didn't get along at all. Their disagreement over the government's size and power is featured in a song in the hit Broadway musical Hamilton.

THOMAS JEFFERSON

ALEXANDER HAMILTON

JACKSONIAN DEMOCRATS

The first two political parties didn't last long. The presidential election of 1820 brought the collapse of the Federalist Party. Soon after, the Democratic-Republican Party split. Many members followed Senator Andrew Jackson, who started a new party in 1828. It later became officially known as the Democratic Party.

Jackson wanted to reduce the federal government's power, to move it away from the rich **elite** of the northeast states and return power to what he considered the common people. He became very popular and, by 1828, won the presidential election by a large majority. Right before his election, a number of states got rid of rules that required white men to own property before they could vote, and Jackson appealed to these white men.

THE WHIG PARTY

When the Democratic-Republicans split, some joined former Federalists and Democrats who didn't like Jackson to form the Whig Party. This political party was a major player in U.S. politics from about 1834 to 1854. William Henry Harrison, the ninth president of the United States, was the first Whig president. Zachary Taylor and Millard Fillmore, the 12th and 13th presidents respectively, were also members of the Whig Party, but by the time Fillmore left office in 1853, the party had split.

ANDREW JACKSON

THE SYMBOL FOR THE DEMOCRATIC PARTY IS A DONKEY. OPPONENTS OF ANDREW JACKSON THOUGHT HE WAS STUBBORN LIKE A DONKEY AND MADE FUN OF HIM. INSTEAD, HE EMBRACED THE IDEA. DEMOCRATS STILL USE THE DONKEY SYMBOL TODAY!

HEAD TO HEAD

While democrats have the donkey symbol, republicans have an elephant for their symbol. The elephant was first used to represent republicans in an 1874 cartoon by Thomas Nast.

9

LINCOLN'S PARTY

The Republican Party started in 1854, when the country was starting to split over slavery. Antislavery leaders created the party, which soon came to replace the Whigs. By the election of 1860, the Democrats split over slavery so much that the Republican candidate, Abraham Lincoln, won the presidency. A number of the Southern states, concerned about slavery, seceded, starting the Civil War.

By the time Lincoln was up for reelection in 1864, the war had been going on for three years. To win, he was going to need votes from both Democrats and Republicans. To get these votes, in 1864, the Republican Party changed its name for a short time and became the National Union Party. Lincoln won the election by a large number of votes.

SNAKES IN POLITICS

During the Civil War, the Democratic Party split into different groups. One group was the War Democrats. They supported the Civil War. A second group was the Copperheads. They wanted to **negotiate** with the Confederate states. Some people thought the Copperheads supported the South. Republicans named them after a snake because people thought they were a danger to the Union.

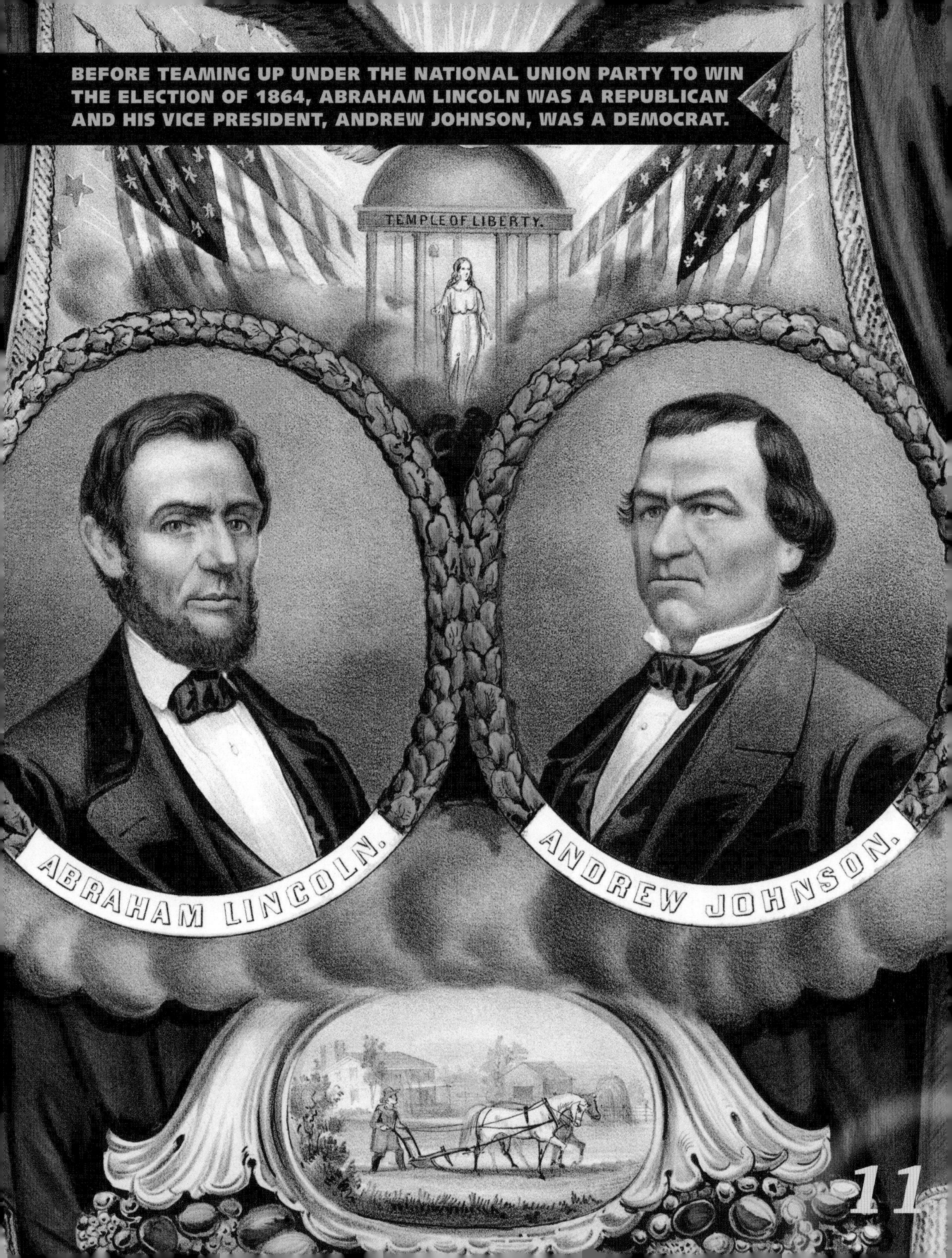

BEFORE TEAMING UP UNDER THE NATIONAL UNION PARTY TO WIN THE ELECTION OF 1864, ABRAHAM LINCOLN WAS A REPUBLICAN AND HIS VICE PRESIDENT, ANDREW JOHNSON, WAS A DEMOCRAT.

AFRICAN AMERICAN SUFFRAGE

After the Civil War ended in 1865, the Democratic Party was largely made up of people who supported businesses, low tariffs, and little government involvement in citizens' lives. Democrats were strongest in southern states that had lost the Civil War. They were upset about the Republican Party's policies after the war.

At this time, the Republican Party supported a strong national government. It supported **Reconstruction** in the South and westward expansion. Republicans were supported by many African American men, who had finally gained the right to vote in 1870, as well as northern businessmen, craftsmen, and skilled workers. This formed a very strong group. African Americans supported the Republican Party in part because the Democratic Party in the South **intentionally** tried to stop them from voting, sometimes supporting violence.

AFTER RECONSTRUCTION ENDED, MANY PEOPLE (ESPECIALLY IN THE SOUTH) TRIED TO KEEP AFRICAN AMERICANS FROM CASTING VOTES. THEY PASSED LAWS TO MAKE IT NEARLY IMPOSSIBLE TO VOTE AND SUPPORTED HATE GROUPS THAT ATTACKED BLACK VOTERS.

BROTHER AGAINST BROTHER

In 1886, two brothers in Tennessee ran against each other for governor. Alfred Taylor was nominated by the Republicans, and his younger brother Robert Taylor was nominated by the Democrats. They were good friends, and they traveled together while they campaigned. The two brothers remained close even after Robert won the election. Alfred was later elected governor of Tennessee in 1920 when he was 72 years old.

THE GREAT DEPRESSION AND THE NEW DEAL

After the Civil War, there was a stretch of Republican presidents starting with Ulysses S. Grant in 1869. Democrat Grover Cleveland took the office in 1885 and then again in 1893, but most of the presidents through the early 1900s were Republicans. In 1929, however, the **Great Depression** hit the country.

It was a very difficult time for America. Many people didn't have jobs. Businesses and banks were failing. Republican president Herbert Hoover thought everything would sort itself out, but things kept getting worse. In 1932, voters elected Democrat Franklin D. Roosevelt.

Roosevelt set out to create jobs and programs that would help bring America out of the Depression. He called this plan the "New Deal." Over time, the economy got better. Roosevelt was elected to three more terms in office.

PEOPLE GOT BY THE BEST THEY COULD DURING THE GREAT DEPRESSION. THOSE WITHOUT HOMES LIVED IN SHEDS OFTEN GROUPED TOGETHER IN WHAT THEY CALLED "SHANTYTOWNS" OR "HOOVERVILLES." PEOPLE USED THIS NAME BECAUSE THEY BLAMED PRESIDENT HOOVER FOR HIS INACTION.

FRANKLIN D. ROOSEVELT

LIBERAL OR CONSERVATIVE?

During the Great Depression, New Deal programs were meant to help people struggling to find and keep jobs. People who believe the government should help with people's problems are generally described as "liberal." Those who believe the government should take a less active approach in people's lives—basically letting society and the economy correct themselves over time— are generally described as "conservative." There are other aspects to this divide as well.

15

SHIFTING PARTY PLATFORMS

The New Deal signaled a major change for both major parties. Before Roosevelt, Democrats tended to believe the government shouldn't be too involved in people's lives or businesses. This changed when voters saw success with the New Deal programs. As America made its way out of the Depression, Democrats gradually became more liberal and started pushing for the government to use its power to create more social programs to help people.

Republicans reacted to the changing Democratic Party by becoming more conservative. They didn't like all the rules and regulations the government was creating and enforcing. In addition, a growing number of conservative southern Democrats disagreed with some of Roosevelt's social policies and the civil rights program of the party.

HEAD TO HEAD

As one of Roosevelt's New Deal projects, construction of the Grand Coulee Dam began in 1933. It employed thousands of men for the eight years it took to build.

LYNDON B. JOHNSON

GRAND COULEE DAM

LET'S DEBATE!

During elections, candidates from all political parties may come together to debate. A political debate is an event where people discuss their views and try to convince voters to support them.

There are two types of political debate. First, people in the same political party debate to try to win their party's nomination, or recommendation, for office. They hope to convince the party members and party leaders that they are the best person for the job.

Second, the chosen party nominees debate each other. They work to convince the public—especially independent and undecided voters—to elect them to the government position. Presidential debates are often shown on television so that voters across America can see the candidates and hear what they have to say.

18

RICHARD NIXON

JOHN F. KENNEDY

THE FIRST TELEVISED PRESIDENTIAL DEBATE WAS IN 1960 BETWEEN DEMOCRAT JOHN F. KENNEDY AND REPUBLICAN RICHARD NIXON. KENNEDY WENT ON TO WIN THE ELECTION.

19

SHAPING THE COURTS

One important job of the U.S. president is nominating judges to the U.S. Supreme Court. This is the highest court in America. It's made up of nine judges, called justices. Usually, Republican presidents nominate conservative judges, and Democratic presidents nominate liberal judges. Sometimes, though, a president will push for a moderate candidate in order to appeal to the public.

For the president's nomination to be accepted, the chosen judge needs the support of the Senate. It takes only a simple majority, meaning just 51 votes out of 100 senators, to **confirm** the nomination. But if a majority of senators are from the opposing political party, it could be difficult for the judge to win enough votes. This is another reason a president might choose to nominate a moderate judge.

SANDRA DAY O'CONNOR WAS SWORN IN AS THE FIRST FEMALE SUPREME COURT JUSTICE IN 1981. PRESIDENT RONALD REAGAN NOMINATED O'CONNOR IN AUGUST, AND SHE WAS CONFIRMED BY A VOTE OF 99 TO 0 IN SEPTEMBER.

SANDRA DAY O'CONNOR

THIRD PARTIES

The Democratic Party and the Republican Party aren't the only options for political parties in America. There are many more, often called third parties because almost all U.S. voters choose the main two. The largest of these parties are the Libertarian Party, the Green Party, and the Constitution Party. These three parties often have candidates running for president, Congress, and local office, too. Because third parties are usually smaller, most are still working on gaining popularity in all 50 states.

Since the rise of the main two U.S. political parties, no third-party candidate has ever won the presidency. Theodore Roosevelt placed second as the Progressive Party candidate in 1912, but since then, the best a third-party candidate has finished is third. Why do you think this is?

HEAD TO HEAD

In 1947, people founded the American Vegetarian Party to promote vegetarianism in America. Members nominated Dr. John Maxwell for the 1948 presidential election, but he never made it onto the **ballot** because

IN 1992, INDEPENDENT CANDIDATE H. ROSS PEROT (CENTER) RAN FOR
PRESIDENT AGAINST THE **INCUMBENT** PRESIDENT, REPUBLICAN GEORGE
H. W. BUSH (LEFT), AND DEMOCRATIC CANDIDATE BILL CLINTON (RIGHT).
CLINTON WON, BUT PEROT WON ALMOST 19 PERCENT OF THE VOTE—MORE
THAN ANY OTHER THIRD-PARTY CANDIDATE IN 80 YEARS.

23

WORKING TOGETHER

The relationship between members of the two parties can be difficult, but Republicans and Democrats don't always disagree. Sometimes they're able to work together. When members of both political parties come together to solve a problem, it's called **bipartisanship**.

In 1990, Democratic and Republican lawmakers came together to pass one of the most important laws reached through bipartisanship. The Americans with Disabilities Act makes it illegal to **discriminate** against someone based on disability. It requires public transportation systems, such as buses, trains, and subways, to be **accessible** with elevators, ramps, and lifts so people who use wheelchairs can get around.

When Democrats and Republicans come together to solve problems, great things can be accomplished. Working together is always more productive than working against each other.

HEAD TO HEAD

"Reaching across the aisle" means that politicians from both major parties come together to reach a compromise. An aisle is a passage between sections of seats.

THE MOON LANDING WOULDN'T HAVE BEEN POSSIBLE WITHOUT
BIPARTISAN COMPROMISE. TODAY, SUPPORT FROM BOTH PARTIES
IS NEEDED FOR NASA TO CONTINUE ITS RESEARCH EFFORTS.

GOING TO THE MOON

On July 20, 1969, at the height of
the space race with the Soviet Union,
American astronauts successfully landed
on the moon. To accomplish this important
feat, Democrats and Republicans had come
together to write bipartisan bills that set up NASA
(National Aeronautics and Space Administration)
in 1958. This is a great example of successful
bipartisanship. NASA still exists today.

25

FAMOUS FLIP-FLOPPERS

Although it's rare, politicians do switch party membership. Sometimes candidates think they have a better chance of winning elections if they switch to the opposite party. Other times they may change their minds about their party's platform. Flip-flopping is sometimes considered a bad thing because it can mean those politicians are inconsistent with their values, and that makes it difficult to know what they really believe in. However, some people change parties to follow their conscience. They may decide their party's changed too much.

Even if you become part of a political party, it's OK to vote for candidates from other political parties if you agree with their values. Learning about candidates and understanding what they believe in is important before you make your choice.

ONE FAMOUS FLIP-FLOPPER WAS ARLEN SPECTER. HE STARTED OUT AS A DEMOCRAT, THEN RAN FOR OFFICE AS A REPUBLICAN IN 1965. AFTER MANY YEARS IN POLITICAL OFFICE AS PART OF THAT PARTY, HE RAN AGAIN AS A DEMOCRAT IN 2009.

REPUBLICANS VS. DEMOCRATS TODAY

The Republican and Democratic Parties today look very different from when they first started. Republicans today tend to support strong nationalism and little government involvement in business. They believe the government should stay out of citizens' lives and states' issues. This is almost the opposite of what Republicans believed back when the party was founded in 1854.

Democrats tend to support the government taking a more active role in helping citizens. They often believe the government should protect people in need and that the government has a responsibility to support equality in America. This, too, is almost the opposite of what Democrats believed when the party was founded in 1828. Both parties will likely continue to change, but as of 2018, there's a deep divide between them.

DEMOCRATS AND REPUBLICANS ARE REPRESENTED BY A DONKEY AND AN ELEPHANT, BUT THEY ALSO ARE ASSOCIATED WITH COLORS. DEMOCRATS ARE ASSOCIATED WITH BLUE WHILE REPUBLICANS USE RED.

LEFT VS. RIGHT

The terms "left" and "right" describe where someone falls on the range of political beliefs. If someone is said to be "on the left," it means that person is more liberal and probably a Democrat. Someone "on the right" is more conservative and probably a Republican. Those who fall in the middle of the spectrum are known as moderates. They still might belong to one party or the other.

29

LOOKING TO THE FUTURE

America's first president, George Washington, warned against having political parties. He felt it would be too easy for politicians to get caught up in fighting each other instead of representing the people. Washington's fears came true when the first parties were established. Today, votes in Congress often follow party lines, meaning that Democrats vote for the Democratic option, and Republicans vote for the Republican option.

Today, the relationship between the two parties is often very **adversarial**. It can be very hard to find common ground. But we know that great things can happen when Democrats and Republicans work together. It's up to voters to choose candidates who will represent their beliefs and work with other politicians to find compromise on behalf of the entire country.

WHAT'S A FILIBUSTER?

In the U.S. Senate, senators sometimes used a method called "filibustering" to block a bill or another measure by preventing a vote on it. In a filibuster, a senator or a group of senators speak for such a long time that no one can vote. The longest solo filibuster on record occurred when Senator J. Strom Thurmond talked for more than 24 hours to try to block the Civil Rights Act of 1957.

GLOSSARY

accessible: The quality of providing access, or the ability to use or enter something.

adversarial: Involving two sides or people who oppose each other.

ballot: A sheet of paper used for voting that lists candidates' names.

bipartisanship: The act of members of two political parties working together.

confirm: To give official approval to something.

constitutional republic: A republic, or a country governed by elected representatives and an elected leader, that has a constitution.

debate: An argument or public discussion. Also, to argue or discuss something.

discriminate: To treat people unfairly based on class, race, religion, or another factor.

elite: The people in a society who are thought to be the greatest.

Great Depression: A period of economic struggle in the United States and much of the world from 1929 to 1939.

incumbent: Having the status of an incumbent, or the holder of an office or position.

intentionally: With intention, or a certain aim or plan.

negotiate: To discuss something formally in order to reach an agreement.

Reconstruction: The period of about 1865 to 1877 in the United States when the southern states were being reestablished and readmitted to the Union after the

INDEX

WEBSITES

Due to the changing nature of Internet links, PowerKids Press has developed an online list of websites related to the subject of this book. This site is updated regularly. Please use this link to access the list: www.powerkidslinks.com/ojah/repdem